SPRING THINGS

A BOOK OF POEMS

written & designed by ROBERT FROMAN
lettering by Ray Barber

Thomas Y. Crowell Company · New York

Library of Congress Cataloging in Publication Data

Froman, Robert, date. Seeing things; book of poems.

SUMMARY: The words of these fifty-one brief poems are
arranged on the pages in shapes appropriate to the subject
of the poem. [1. Concrete poetry, American] I. Title.
PZ8.3.F928Se   811'.5'4   73-18494   ISBN 0-690-00291-2

Manufactured in the United States of America

ISBN 0-690-00291-2

1 2 3 4 5 6 7 8 9 10

To
Elizabeth

CONTENTS

A SEEING POEM

A SEEING POEM HAPPENS WHEN WORDS TAKE A SHAPE THAT HELPS THEM TO TURN ON A LIGHT IN SOMEONE'S MIND

QUIET SECRET

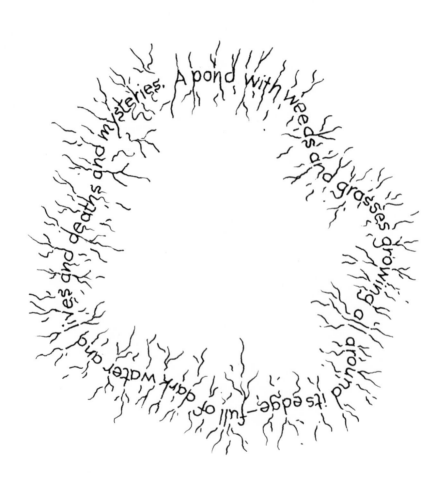

A pond with weeds and grasses growing all around its edge—full of dark water and lives and deaths and mysteries.

WHEN BIRDS REMEMBER

Birds in a tight
cloud flying off
on an important
errand they had
almost forgotten about.

SUDDEN
SILENCE

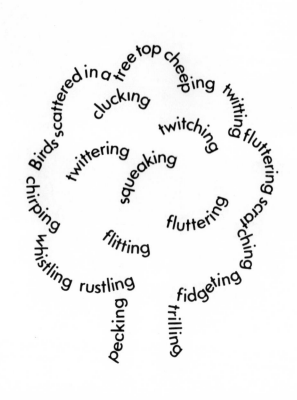

Birds scattered in a tree top cheeping twitting fluttering scratching

clucking

twitching

twittering squeaking

chirping

fluttering

whistling rustling

flitting

fidgeting

pecking trilling

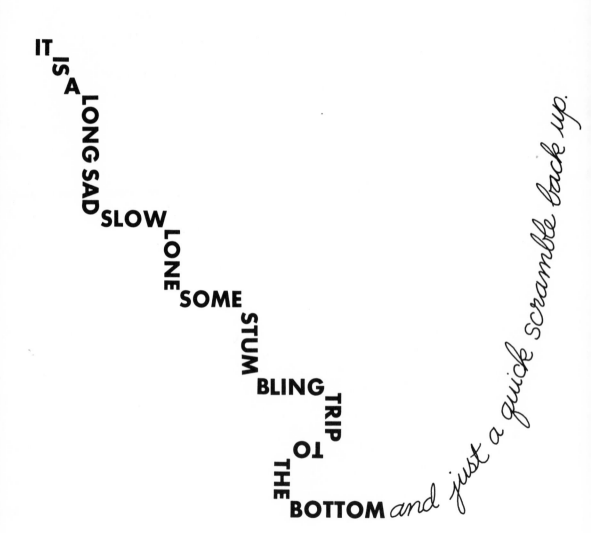

IT IS A LONG SAD SLOW LONESOME STUMBLING TRIP TO THE BOTTOM *and just a quick scramble back up.*

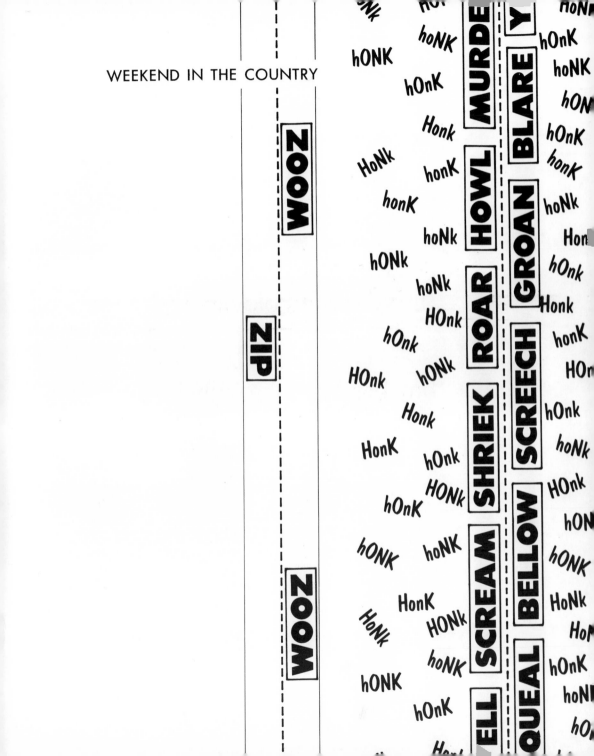

WET BEAUTY

The rain raining

Then the wind blowing

Tiny brooklets through the air.

BOX OF WORDS

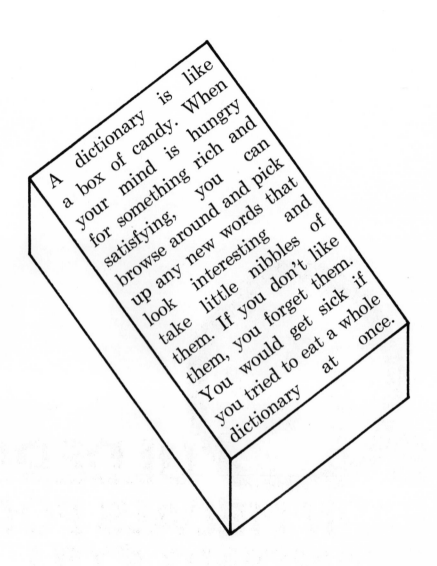

A dictionary is like a box of candy. When your mind is hungry for something rich and satisfying, you can browse around and pick up any new words that look interesting and take little nibbles of them. If you don't like them, you forget them. You would get sick if you tried to eat a whole dictionary at once.

BOULDERS
EARN MEDALS FOR
STANDING STILL

DEAD TREE

YOU LIVED A LONG TIME TREE. NOW YOU STAND AWHILE, BARE AND ALONE A MONUMENT TO YOUR PAST, UNTIL YOU ARE READY TO FALL AND BECOME FOOD FOR YOUR FUTURE.

LISTEN, GRASS, TAKE IT EASY. DON'T GROW TOO TALL. THEY'LL JUST BRING IN A MOWING MACHINE AND CUT YOU DOWN SHORT.

SEE? I TOLD YOU THEY WOULD.

A COBWEB MAY LOOK MESSY BUT TO SOME SPI-DER IT IS HOME

A FROZEN LEAP ACROSS THE WATER

SHIVERS
GETS THE
THE ROAD
HOT HOT HOT
WORLD IS HOT
WHOLE WIDE
EVERYTHING IN THE
HOT AND ABSOLUTELY
THE GROUND IS
AIR IS HOT AND
IS HOT AND THE
WHEN THE SUN

WALL WALK

THIN
WALL.
STEEP   FALL.
STEP
CARE-
FULLY
ARMS   OUT.
TIP   TIP
BUT
NOT
TOO
MUCH
TIP.
BAL-
ANCE.
AH.
MADE IT.

DIS APPEARER
RE

Duck on the water.

He's gone!

Where?

Oh.

Diving duck.

again.

Here he comes

A time for listening to what the world has to say.

MADNESS

I'M 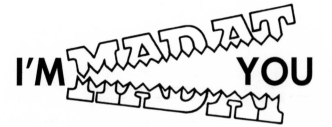 YOU

YOU'RE  ME

WE'RE MAD AT THEM

SNAP!

No sign of life above ground yet,

But down below the roots are waking,

Stretching down down down

Green time is coming.

Soon.

HELP!

NOBODY IN THE WHOLE WIDE WORLD LIKES ME. WORTHLESS, USELESS, HOPELESS. IT'S BECAUSE I'M NO GOOD, ROTTEN, GO AWAY AND LEAVE ME ALONE IN MY MISERY.

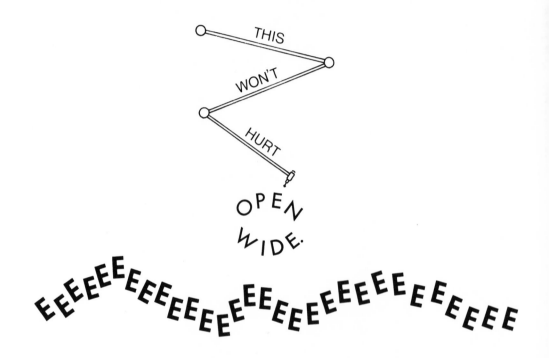

THIS
WON'T
HURT

OPEN
WIDE.

EEEEEEEEEEEEEEEEEEEEEEEEEEEEEEEEEEE

WELL.

IT DIDN'T.

MUCH.

SHOO GAME

Nice dirty tablecloth.

Great browsing for flies.
Or are they playing some kind of checkers?

PICTURE WINDOW YOU'RE VERY IMPRESSIVE, BUT IT'S MORE FUN

A PEEP-HOLE. TO SPY THROUGH

CONJUGATION

ISLAND: A LAND OF IS SURROUNDED BY WAS AND WILL BE AND SHOULD BE AND CANNOT BE AND SHALL TRY TO BE AND SEEMS TO BE AND NEVER CAN BE AND LOOKS LIKE BEING AND GETTING TO BE AND MAY BE AND OUGHT TO BE AND COULD HAVE BEEN AND WOULD BE AND HAS BEEN AND

23

GRAVEYARD

Great,
high, billowing cloud,
Brilliant with sunlight
On a hot summer day.
Magnificent to
behold.

And for a bonus—
the cool caress of
your shadow.

		Cal	en	dar,	you	work
hard	to	cut	some	thing	in	to
lit	tle	pie	ces.	Have	you	ev
er	tried	to	find	out	just	what
you	are	cut	ting	up?		

AUTOMATIC ELEVATOR

You
stare
at
the
blank
door.

It
slides
open.
You
step
inside.

The
door
slides
shut
and you
stare.

It
slides
open.
You
step
out

into someplace else.

A SLIVER MOON

ONLY THE WEDGE OF SKY CARVED OUT
BY THE KNIVES OF THE BUILDINGS.

ONLY THE RIM OF MOON CARVED
OUT BY THE LIGHT OF THE SUN.

IN A
SLI
VER
SKY

ONLY THE

ICE RAW
SLICE STIFF COLD
BLEAK
CHILL
ROCK
CUT HARD

MELTING
ENLOSS
SLUSH
DRIP
SLOSH
TURN
DRIP
DERTI
SLOSH
ENZOLTSH
SLUSH
DRIP
HP
PH
MUD

DUSTY, NOSY

A shaft of sunlight
Dancing with dust.

Sniff it.
Sharp.
Scratchy.
Sneezy.

VACANT LOT

We call it vacant.

It bears no house.

All it has in it

Are 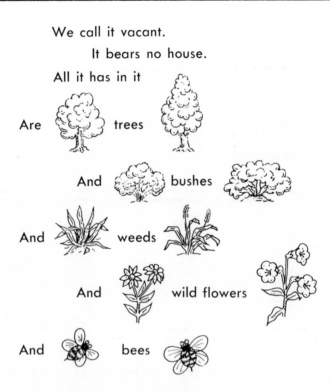 trees

And bushes

And weeds

And wild flowers

And bees

And ants and grasshoppers and beetles and butterflies and wasps
and crickets and mosquitoes and gnats and flies and dragonflies
and sparrows and robins and warblers and chickadees and orioles
and mourning doves and cardinals and swallows and mockingbirds
and wood thrushes and woodpeckers and bluebirds and meadowlarks
and earthworms and centipedes and millipedes and salamanders
and toads and newts and snakes and lizards and mice and moles
and voles and rabbits and woodchucks and skunks and weasels
and cats and dogs and rocks and pebbles and earth and air and

Ticket
seller
in a
glass
cage

Ticket
taker
at the
door

And in the darkness they guard
Sometimes
An empty blah
And
Sometimes

SUMMER WALK

Sun on the sidewalk,
Warm to my bare feet.
Sun on the blacktop,

DROUGHT

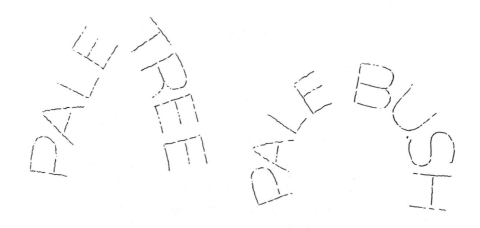

PALE TREE PALE BUSH PALE GRASS

DUST IS KING TODAY

BRIGHT TREE
BRIGHT BUSH
BRIGHT GRASS

NOW REIGNS THE CLEANSING RAIN

WAVE

WAVE WAVE

WAVE WAVE WAVE

FOAM FOAM FOAM

SAND SAND SAND SAND SAND SAND SA
SAND SAND SAND SAND SAND SANDSAN
SAND SAND SAND SAND SANDSANDSANDS
ANDSANDSANDSAND SAND SANDSANDS
NDSANDSANDSANDS SNSANDSAND SAND
DSANDSANDS SANDSANDSANDS
SANDSANDSA CLAM NDSANDSANDS
AND SANDSA SHELL DSANDSANDSA
NDSANDSANDSA SANDSANDSA
SANDSANDSA SANDSANDSANDS
ANDSAND SANDSANDSANDSA
NDSANDSANDSANDSA STARFISHNOSAN
SANDSANDSANDSA STARFISH DSAND SAND
SANDSANDSANDS STAR NDSANDSANDS
SANDSANDSAND SANDSANDSANDS
SANANDSANDSANDS SANDSANDSANDS
NO AND N SANDSANDSANDSAND
ND D N A

HARD
GREY
ROCK

SAND SAND SAND SAND SAND SAND SANDSAN
NDSANDSANDSAND SAND SAND SANDSAND
DSANDSAND SAND CLAM ANDSANDSANDS
SANDSANDSAND SAND SHELL DSANDSANDSA
ANDSAND SAND S SANDSANDSAN
NDSANDSANDS D SANDSANDSAC
DSANDSANDSA SAND SANDANDSANDS
SAND SAND SAND D ANDSANDSANDSAN
ANDSP D SANDSANDSANDSAN
NDSA PEBBLES SAND SAND SANDSANDS
BSA BBLES NOSANDSANDSANDS
SAND SAND SA NDSANDSANDSANDS
SAND SAND S SANDSANDSAND SAND S
SANDSANDSANDSAND ANDSANDSANDSA
ANDSANDSANDS SANDSANDSANDSANDS
ANDSANDSANDSANDSANDS NDSANDSANDS
SANDSANDSANDSANDSANDSANDS ANOSANDSANDS
N N ANDANDSANDSANDSANDS
A D D N N S
N S D O O N S D
A D N A D
N D

TYPEWRITANGER

Whack, crack, smack, rack, tack,
CLANGK!
    Hackety, thwackety, flackety, clackety,
CLANGK!
    Somebody's talking mean on that
typewriter.

TWO SNOWS

When snow
flakes drift
down on you
from above
they are soft
as kisses.

BUT WHEN THE WIND DRIVES
THEM AT YOU SIDE
WAYS, THEY CUT
LIKE FROZEN
KNIVES.

WHEE

_PACKED SNOW STEEP HILL FAST SLED_____

In the road a pile of

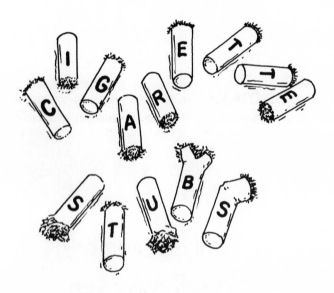

Makes the mud
Look clean and sweet.

Piece of burnt wood.
Smells like

smoke

Only a memory.
The fire is over.

HOW TO

WHEN THINGS ARE TOO MUCH AND YOU MAKE UP YOUR MIND TO GET RID OF THEM, GET YOURSELF A

PUSHBROOM

HUFFS GLOOM
FAULTS PEEVES GROUCHES SCOFFS
BLAHS CRABBIES ENEMIES
NAGNAGS SULKS TAUNTS UGHS HORNIES
PEEVES GRIMLIES CHIDES
GRUMPS SLURS

Sit still, little toad.

All still.

Do not twitch.

Do not blink.

Be invisible.

And then give one great

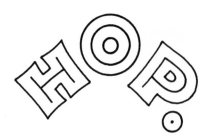

WINTER
WOODS BARE
TWIGGY
EASY TO SEE
THROUGH

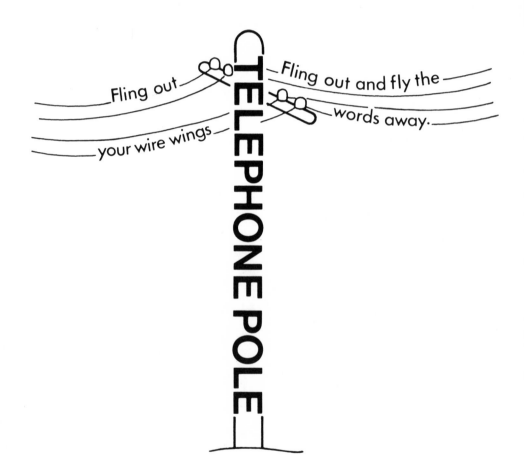

Fling out your wire wings

TELEPHONE POLE

Fling out and fly the words away.

HALT!

Listen here, slippery!

Stop stretching your legs like that.

Are you planning to run away?

Now LOOK!

You've got others doing it, too

ABANDONED

Once upon a time, House,
You were neat and tidy.
Which way do you like it best?
Is it interesting to go to pieces?

POWER HOUSE

Whirlllllll Whirlllllll Whirlllllll Whirlllll
SpinnnnnSpinnnnnSpinnnnnSpinn
HummmmmmHummmmmm Hum
HummmmmmHummmmmm Hum
Whirlllllll Whirlllllll Whirlllllll Whirlllll
SpinnnnnSpinnnnnSpinnnnnSpinn
HummmmmmHummmmmm Hum
HummmmmmHummmmmm Hum
Whirlllllll Whirlllllll Whirlllllll Whirlllll
SpinnnnnSpinnnnnSpinnnnnSpinn

We cannot see
What goes around
Inside your thick, blank walls,
Power house.
But when we touch you,
We can FEEL IT

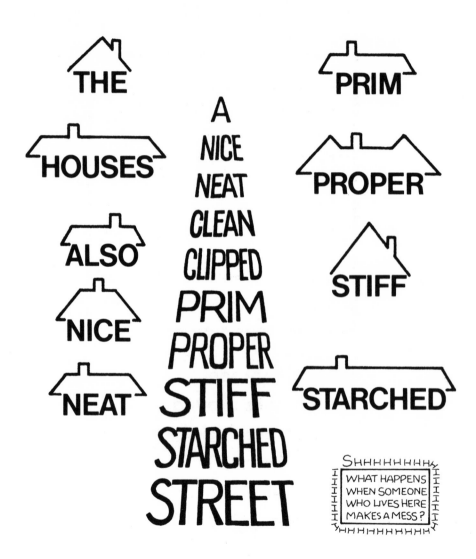

THE

PRIM

HOUSES

A
NICE
NEAT
CLEAN
CLIPPED
PRIM
PROPER
STIFF
STARCHED
STREET

PROPER

ALSO

STIFF

NICE

NEAT

STARCHED

SHHHHHHHHH
WHAT HAPPENS
WHEN SOMEONE
WHO LIVES HERE
MAKES A MESS?

WITH THEM

COULD FLY OFF

I WISHED THAT I

INTO THE SKY

FLY OFF

SOME CROWS

ONCE I SAW

SKY DAY DREAM

ABOUT THE AUTHOR

Robert Froman says that the poems in this book "began as a sort of freewheeling haiku." The next stage was when the words of the poems moved on the page, taking the shape of the things they described and providing the reader with an innovative way of "seeing things."

Mr. Froman is the author of more than twenty books, for readers of all ages, most of them in the areas of science and mathematics. This is his second book of poetry for young readers. The *New York Times* said of the first, *Street Poems,* "Words tumble and whirl across the page, leap-frogging exuberantly over the horizon of the conventional sentence . . . the poems are simple, witty unities, and they are fun."

Born in Big Timber, Montana, and educated at Reed College in Oregon, Mr. Froman now lives in Tomkins Lake, New York, with his wife, Elizabeth Hull Froman, who is also a writer of books for children.